Heart of a Queen

Poetry and Prose from the Soul

Unless otherwise indicated, all scriptural quotations are from the *New King James Version* of the Bible.

'Heart of a Queen – Poems and Prose from the Soul'

Published by

Write Right Publications
PO Box 1194
Merchantville, NJ 08109-1194

ISBN 978-0-09856627-3-8

Copyright © 2013

Nina C. Brewton

All rights reserved.

Reproduction of text in whole or in part without the express written consent by the author is not permitted and is unlawful according to the 1976 United States Copyright Act.

Printed in the United States of America

Cover Design by Stan Davis for Mann Made LLC, Atlanta, GA

Cover Photo by B. Breezy for The Studio Concept, Atlanta, GA

Styling by Molly Jones (www.iammollyjones.com) and Yadida (www.yadiyda.com)

Back cover photo by Sheora M. Harris for SheUnique Photography

Styling by Up Next Boutique, Portsmouth, VA

Dear Friend, Lover, Reader:

I have poured my heart into these pages.

I decided to share this small collection of poetry – of my thoughts and ideas – in hopes of inspiring you to see others' hearts of from my perspective. I also aspire to assist others with learning how to better manage their own emotions. Perhaps you'll recognize a piece of yourself in my words.

As I have grown up and grown older, I finally find myself becoming more comfortable with the person that God created me to be. One major part of my personality that has often frustrated me through the years is my wide open and gracious heart. I have lived and loved large. I have given those in need the shirt and coat off my back *and* a ride to their next destination. I have shared this love people who continuously failed to reciprocate.

While this kind of love and affection has often left me shirtless, coatless and low on gas, I have always trusted that it was the right way to behave. I remember when giving my time and treasure made me feel weak and vulnerable. I often found myself feeling hurt and alone.

I've grown to understand that a lot of people have simply never learned how to truly love. They've been hurt, scarred and jaded; this has led them to keep people at a distance. These behaviors, these thoughts, have sometimes caused them to hurt others, often unconsciously. They personified the idea that misery loves company. It can be difficult for people to recognize how their actions hurt others and themselves.

Does this mean I am perfect? No. I have broken hearts. I can always be more gracious and loving. As a woman growing in God's will, I recognize the importance of graciousness. I am learning to see things from others' vantages. I am walking confidently in the freedom that comes from extending grace to friends and family; indeed, to everyone. I thank God that people know they can depend on me no matter what.

And so, to those who have called me friend over the years but have shown me less than the love I deserved… *smiling at God* …don't see me as weak. I am far from lonely. And even though the actions of others still hurt at times, I have all that I need. Most importantly, I have the grace of God & His love in my heart that allows me to pour the same grace & love onto others who have need.

With all of that being said – I♥YOU!!! (Yes, even you…)

Nina

A Few Haikus
(and stuff…)

Between Me and You 2004

Time and distance race
To see which one can drive me
Crazy the fastest

Acceptance 2011

Like life in the spring
Perfect timing, as purpose
Made its way to me

Failure 2013

One's failure to love
Is a tree which yields no fruit
Leaving all hearts starved

Fruit of the Spirit 2013

Plucking my last nerve
Is like plucking my branches
Here, have some more fruit

Today Feels Like

Today feels like jazz
Crisp air
I inhale melodies
Exhale rhythms
Walking on riffs
Staccato in hips
Arms as bows, swinging
Playing slow

Today feels like jazz
Trees as trumpets
Dancing with black & white keys
Breeze, the rich voice of Cassandra
Sun shining bright like Louie's trumpet
Puffy clouds, smoke in the old room.

Today feels like jazz

BEAM 2013

…then the sun showed
Kissing me, deeply.
Lighting me from inside out
Driving clouded melancholy from my heart,
Bringing my mind peace.

Just like that it began, a rhythm.
Through me, then, there shone a
Love like the one you lost,
Only real,
And I give it to you with every smile.
You are left, inspired, to kiss another, ever so deeply
Beginning with the sunshine in your eyes

In Love & Broken Hearted

A Night of You 1999
(A Dream…)

I love you

It's cold out here without you

I dreamed I made love to you last night

The things we gave each other…

It all mattered

And then you were gone and still here

Missing you, missing you…

I woke up wanting you

Really

Wanting…

I woke up lonely

Should you have left me lonely?

A Walk in Your Shoes 1999

Tonight I watched you walk away, and I hurt…

But this isn't about me.

Though tonight I wore one of your shirts trying to imagine how it feels to be a stylish, fine Black man who feels trapped in this place in this dungeon where we were born, trying to escape.

I watched *lovejones* and laughed at the parts that were funny, while sitting on the edge of the bed, remembering the first night that began our love…

Tonight I listened to *Giant Steps*, over and over, trying to really love Coltrane and pay homage…the way you do, sometimes all night long.

I put your oil on my body and realized how sweet all of this really is…

One. Two. One. Two. Three. Four.

I even smoked a cigarette, yes, while imagining how you feel while loving me—misunderstood—yet—loving me still…

Tonight I tried on your shoes, not to understand your style, but to understand you

The man I love

I imagined myself through your eyes

I considered your feelings, knowing that you may never understand mine.

I also played Donny tonight, while you were gone. The same way I did when I wrote about my ideal man, and how, "he understands the spiritual world and takes that into consideration, on my bad days, when I may be under attack of the enemy."

You are the friend I've wanted for a long time, even in my youth.

The one who will dance with me, just because he feels like dancing

Whether there's music or none

How he will try to make me laugh through my tears – and succeed

But this is not about me, it's about you

And so, I touched myself tonight to try and feel what you feel when you put your hands on me, and make me feel so…

So many more things went through my mind while I was in your shoes

The one who gives so much and never gets in return

I saw that tonight, as I lay thinking about you and how you make me feel…

Kiss My Lips 1999

(It's beautiful, as I open up to you)

It's beautiful

The way your kisses expose drops of gold beneath this hue of henna

And it is pure…

All that is no longer hidden

The moon is full behind these clouds that have not

Dropped

Cats

     Nor dogs

At this time   though I can smell it coming

Its sweet like

The taste of your letting me know how much you enjoy all of your time spent with me

You put your lips to mine

And wherever else they are beckoned

Yes, sweet like the

    R

      A

        I

          N

That fell just hours before we looked to the east and

F   I   R   E   burned the day across the sky

Kiss my lips as if you've

Never tasted the cool sweetness of a grape's delectable juices

As the soft core falls across your tongue

It is made warm, as if it has fallen across mine as well…

Think of Me 2000

Think of me when it rains

For with every drop I seem to care for you more and more…

As you sit and watch the rain fall to the ground, or wherever it may land

Think of me

Each drop is numbered

As you estimate how many there are

Multiply that number by a million and that will give you an idea of how much

I care for you

Think of me when it rains

Think warm thoughts

So that even if I can't be there by your side

The thought of my being there will keep you from the cold

I am with you

Think of me when it rains
Let's take a walk together
Let the soft beads of water fall down upon us
And cleanse us

To dry off we'd hide under an oak tree
Until the clouds go by
Hold me in your arms
I'm with you
Always

So don't wish the rain away
Each roll of thunder is the sound of my heart
Beating for you

Each drop of rain
Indicates the thousands of tears
I'd cry

If you were to ever leave me

So think of me…

My Ideal 2000

My ideal is one who is not ashamed to declare his love for our Savior Jesus and loves the life that the Lord hath giveth…

To appreciate verses like "We gather gold from the evening sun and it's heavenly hues/and we don't have a thing to lose…"

Or he might sing a song by Donny in his own rendition.

My ideal understands the spiritual world and takes that into consideration on my "bad days" when I may be under attack. He'll anoint me with oil in prayer, "Back up devil, back up."

He's someone who could study and master the chords that Stevie could see and do the same understanding Bach or Mozart.

We would discuss how music has lost its creativity, it's passion and it's…

I might say, "For which I love, stand, fall or die," and he could speak on a number of things that might move him to feel this way; still keeping Him first.

He would announce that "For Christ I live and for Christ I die, but Lord my people struggle, so God please give me the strength to fight this natural war as well…"

He would have made Shakespeare cringe while reading the Psalms as the poetry it is.

Literary intellectuals would cry and give their lives to the Lord because he would tell the Word like they have been longing for something their whole lives. They may have never heard it in the ritualistic mass of the Roman Catholic Church.

He would have a philosophy for life and maybe that philosophy would change from day to day.

He is entitled to change right?

"I am open and willing to change."

Because he realized that it's going to happen anyway so he might as well be prepared for it.

I will accept it with him—because he is my ideal

man

lover

friend

Among other things

Play Brother, Play 2000

(for keith, james, and 'trane)

He plays

He plays a long golden horn

Sounds come from within

To soothe my mind

Body

And soul

But he can do that

With brown fingers stretched endlessly along the golden horn

Like tantalizing kisses

Dancing   across the golden hues of

My body

He plays music

OOOH, that beautiful music

I need him

Just to listen to all day long

Whether it be the horn that I listen to or the smooth subtle tone of his

Deep voice

He plays – And yes people listen

But can you feel it

Do you feel it (deep inside)   the way I do

WHOO!! Play brother play

If I need to you know I'll pay

What's the price   mytimemyearsmylove

If none of that I'll give you all of me

You make mad love

Passionate love the way you play

With you and only you I want to make love throughout the day

Make me sing about you

Make me feel your rhythm inside of me
set me free

Brotha play some more   don't ever stop

It is my only pleasure to hear you play
Pleasure

playbrothaplaybrothaplaybrothaplay

Alone With Self and Consequences
2001

I think I'll sit atop trees to cry these tears of mine so that people may say,

"Oh, it's raining again" instead of, "damn, she's crying again?"

I sometimes wish that a thousand bugs would crawl across my skin

Leaving small bumps as evidence of their feeding so that I could think of that and not of you…

I want to drink until I black out so that I may have no remembrance of the look in your eyes the first time we met.

I wish that scientist and surgeons would all come together to perform a revolutionary procedure removing all memories of you and me that are still creeping around in my mind…

I would like to be circumcised so that I may never touch myself again in an attempt to relive how it felt to make love to you…

I at times desire to have my hearing lost so that I cannot hear when people ask if I've seen you, or how have you been? Because I DON'T KNOW!!!!!!

I want to have my hands removed so that I might not reach for you…as you walk on by…

How Many Times Can I Say? 2001

Ain't gonna stop

Won't stop   don't wanna stop

Loving you

Reminiscing of you

Loving you

Wanting you

Ain't gonna stop (should I stop?)

Can't stop

Remembering how you loved me

Can't believe that you stopped, wanna stop loving me

Ain't gonna look at the sun the same no more.

It ain't the same

Won't be the same

Don't shine

Won't shine

Don't shine the same on me

Ain't gonna smell the sweet smell of rain

Been raining all the time

Like my roof done fell down

And down come rain

On my head

On my parade

Been rained out but the smell ain't the same

Ain't the same

Ain't never gonna be the same

Don't smell the same

Will I still love the rain

The way I did when we used to sit inside out of the rain

Ain't no more sitting wit' you 'cause it ain't no you

Lovin' me

Lovin' me, I love you

Could I ever be?

The one you still love

Won't be

Can't be

'Cause you don't want me to be

You say you

Love me

Don't love me

Ain't never loved me

Want me

Don't want me

Can't have me

Scared around me

Confused wit' me

Confused without me

Don't know whether you love me or hate me

Well, there's no doubt in my mind

No question in my heart

I love you

Want you

Love you

Want to be with you

I love you

Can't get over you

I love you

Can't get over the fact that you're over me

The sun don't shine the same

The sky ain't blue

Though it is in my blue, green red with fire eyes

Blue green red

Red green blue

Green blue red

Fire red in my eyes

Green with envy

Blue from love

Tears of love

Mood

Done lost

Love

Not known anymore

Tears of love

Love has died

Mood done lost

Life

Done lost

Love

Done turned blue

You don't want me

But I need you…

Of How…God Is 2004

The trouble with me used to be

That

I couldn't find the words to express

How beautiful he was   to me

How much I loved him

How WAAAAAAARM I felt when he was near

And how a chill filled my lungs

Filled my blood stream…

My heart

When he was away

The wind never blew so cold

I.

Couldn't.

Live.

Without.

Him…

But I

Just couldn't seem

To tell him…

Now…

He's gone…

He's left me…

Perhaps forever…

Maybe 'til later

I guess I won't know…until later…

I've learned to not dwell on what is no longer

Nor

What could be

Definitely not

What I feel should be

It's not up to me

But finally

I don't think of him the same anymore

My body no longer

Yeeeeaaarrns

For his presence

For his fragrance

For his…

For him

My thoughts of him have been turned into prayers

Where I once wanted him to share in my misery

I now pray only for his happiness

For his prosperity

Peace

In his heart

Rest

For his mind

I'm no longer concerned about his hand in mine

I love him…and do sometimes say so…

But I'm sure by now…he knows

In all of my thoughts about him

My focus has changed

Blessed to have been loved by him

I'm blessed to be loved by Him

Having had him in my life is a constant reminder of

Exactly

How God is

How good God is

How merciful God is

How loving God is

How patient God is

How truly unworthy I am to be loved by (h)Him

How grateful I am to be loved by Him

I can be easy to give up on

As he did

But He never has

But that's just how…God is

Out From Within the Deep 2009

(For Dwayne)

I have seen his eyes penetrated by the sunlight

Those beams captured by dark places in his mind

He walked out of my life years ago for reasons that were his

Leaving behind God & the vision that He had given him

He left the poetry that we shared

The conviction in his words now mere whispers

He'd misplaced the rhythm in his speech that God used to draw people to Himself

He once spoke of Love freely and gave it effortlessly

I felt that he'd remain in "the deep" forever

Today, through his voice, I imagined the light in his eyes that shone from within his heart...the darkness that had consumed him shattered as music eliminates silence

I heard freedom in his smile as he spoke of the God we love

BAD HABITS 2010

I understand why he's so scared

THAT love

That love ran deep

It's still in his veins

Bad habits are hard to break

Although adopting them as

Part of you

Is easy to get into

Like taking a hit for the first time

Knowing…

…addiction is real

Knowing…

That you could get use to the taste

The smell

The longing for it

That thing runs so deep

A recovering addict can't commune with the saints

Just a sip will have him backsliding

Just the sound of her name

Triggers memories marking the beginning of the obsession

Like sin
It's still in his heart

I understand why he's scared

He's afraid of wanting what he worked so hard at getting over

I understand...

...I am too

Weather the Storm 2012

We collided

Fast and free

As storms do

I, high and dry out of the Midwest,

You, laying low on the east coast

Neither meteorologist nor cupid could have predicted

And neither did we

Eyes wide open to the colors on the horizon

Watching each other from across the room

Who knew that our fronts would collide creating a storm like no other?

I, hoping my sunny smile would break through the clouds

Your eyes dark, holding back nightmares like pending rain

You still keep watch as night falls

Sleepless

The stillness of the air

The calm before the storm forbids your sleep

You're the watchman

I often wondered, in your midnight, as I lay dreaming of blue skies

Did you see the destruction coming?

Did the darkness of the night bring daydreams?

Maybe you saw that we wouldn't weather the storm

We didn't trust that we could dance in the rain *together*

In unison

Step by step

Matching the rhythm of each drop

Swaying with the breeze

Instead, we loved hard

Energies clashing

Igniting lightning strikes

Our love sparked wild fires

Passion burning fervently

Consuming everything in its path

Leaving behind earth so fertile

We could feed nations from its fruit

But you ran for cover

Running when my winds blew too hard

Carrying emotions you weren't prepared to weather

Another storm, on the horizon

I didn't recognize that your habit of leaving

Pennies tossed about the bedroom floor

Was evidence of the hail storms that had bruised your heart

No insurance adjuster could add up the damage

But I

I wanted to melt your chilled heart

My love luminous rainbows

Vibrant colors painted by rogue sunrays shine through

You as daggered 'cicles clinging dangerously from rooftops

There's beauty locked within that cold, hard core

And just like a tornado you

Rush in

Unannounced

Turning my world upside down in the most beautiful way

Tumultuously

You love me

And leave

Your presence fleeting like the seasons

Until the next time our fronts collide again

The Battle Within

I See It 1992

I don't know what it is that makes me so beautiful
But I see it
It may be there once a week
Or maybe even everyday for a whole week
It come sand it goes
It changes with the weather
I don't know what it is but it makes me feel better
Maybe it's in my shape
No really, it's more than that
Maybe it's my beautiful brown eyes
Maybe it's simply because I'm Black
I guess I'll never know what it really is
Maybe it's my full lips
I don't know what it is
All I know is
I see it

Sometimes (reckless) 2001

I can't believe that I considered going to the club
tonight instead of this open mic
Sometimes…

I never thought I'd come here tipsy
But I like to drink
And I'd be lying if I said I ain't been drinking tonight
I wish I'd stayed drug free sometimes
I've not always been
I've even craved weed lately
At times but…

Back to drinkin'…

I get to drinkin' and drivin'
Sometimes…
I'm not the only one though
I had to go as far as praying my way home onetime…

I like to…well…um…forget what I was 'bout to say
sometimes

I love to feel the comfort of others

Sometimes…

I like to feel the throbbin' of brothas
Sometimes…
I wish I wasn't saved

Sometimes…

Then the guilt wouldn't be so strong…

Sometimes I like to more than act like I have no home training
Sometimes putting my foot in someone's ass is not the only thing I'd like to do
Sometimes I wish I would just let loose and bust a bitch in their lip…and keep bustin' and Bustin' and bustin' all over their head until…sometime…

Sometimes I wish I could be unlike myself
Steal a pair of shoes
And again, kick a bitch's ass…

I like to send cat calls to my brothas from building to building or across the street
"Yo shawty, what yo name ils?"
Sometimes I'm country

Sometimes…
I wish this lust didn't burn at my flesh
Sometimes I wish I could suck a dick and fuck a dick ménage a toi
Let that freak in me go free

I wish I could follow the will of God…

Then, sometimes

Wild fantasies invade my mind
I wish I would wear short skirts wit' no panties
Touchin' dicks, kissin' lips

Shake my ass down a pole and get paid good money
to do so in another woman's face
Giving her pleasure

Sometimes I wish I could decipher your actions
Sometimes I wish I could control my emotions

Instead I've been known to throw beer bottles
And drop plenty of tears
And cuss
And well…

I don't finish my poems
Sometimes…

These other poets make me not only want to burn my notebook
But they make me want to never use words again
Even when thinking, I sometimes want to just think with pictures

Sometimes…

And then, I remember the Love that has been given to me that makes all things new

Sometimes…

I have to remind myself that

I am new a new creature

Confused at 0315 2001

Right now I want my skin scrubbed with *African Mud Salt* from the *Body Shop*. I did that for myself today, but I want someone else to do the scubbin' for me.

I'm depressed

I want someone to wash my hair with peppermint/tea tree oil shampoo and I'm not asking Erin, because she's my hairdresser, she gets paid to do so. And though she does a good job on my hair, she just doesn't exactly have the strength that I'm looking for.

Depressed

I'm not tired, but I'd like to leave here and maybe sleep until whatever is next happens…

I've already listened to the whole quiet storm and requested songs that weren't played though I guess it isn't really THAT important. It's not like I was dedicating Charlie Wilson music to anyone in particular and even if I was, he probably wouldn't be listening, and if he was listening, he wouldn't acknowledge that he heard. Not to me anyway…well, enough about him.

I want to bathe until I feel the freshest that I ever have in my life.

I want to be inspired

Should I say motivated to write about something other than…you know…

Him

Here I go again…this is about me

Not him

I want to walk around smelling nothing but sweet fragrances all day long. Whether it's me, or the absence of this can next to me with garbage in it.

Something's got to give.

Because right now, I'm lonely and I want to just leave and get my own damn peppermint shampoo and wash these twist out of my own hair, since I have no strong hands to rub my scalp

Is this becoming a poem about the absence of he, or not of any he in particular?

This is a poem about me

About how I wish I could shake this feeling that my mother has attempted to describe for years and I could never understand. How this feeling could drive her into a continuing role in a hospital drama…

And she told me to seek help this weekend. While she was drinking her first alcoholic beverage in 3 years. Not that drinking was ever her problem…she hardly did drink, but it was something to have. The idea of a drinking problem that is…

And I don't know the exact words to describe what it is that is consuming my mind

AND I'M A DAMN POET!!!!

Maybe I'm not after all.

I think I'm gonna leave and get that shampoo, go home and take a bath with vinegar in it to feel fresh, wash my hair, file my nails, rub my own damn feet, and lather myself down with cocoa butter just before spraying myself with whatever fragrance I want…

I FEEL FILTHY

I AM DEPRESSED AND CAN STILL SMILE AND SMILE AND SMILE AND SMILE AND SMILE AND SMILE AND EVEN LAUGH A LOT

And mean it…

Did I forget to mention the tears that somehow have managed to not fall and oh, I feel like crying…AND CRYING AND CRYING AND CRYING AND CRYING.

And I might real soon…as a matter of fact, I'm sure I will…soon

And if someone is around to experience this, they'll ask why I'm crying and I won't have one word to tell them.

It's not one thing that has me feeling like this

Lack of friends (true friends, that's called loneliness), fucked up finances (on account of my own stupidity), bad health (thanks to my own stupidity) and this green uniform that does nothing for me…

And this smell?! Because the powder I thought would cover the smell of nothingness that surrounded me, but it only smells bad and the smell of the trashcan next to me (I need to get some air freshener for this office.)

Is this a poem, or..?????

I Am Beautiful 2009

Grateful for my beauty and for God allowing me to be who I am...
I am not perfect.

Physically, I'm overweight and my skin is sensitive and dry, and there's more...too much to mention really...

Mentally, I tend to be too emotional, others can see it at times and even I can see it on occasion when I know I've taken something too far...

Spiritually, yeah, there is ALWAYS more that I can give the Lord. Always...It is amazing the revelation u receive when u actually READ your Bible and EXPECT to hear from the Lord. The simplest things become so profound. If only I'd read more/listen more/see more...of You, Lord.

I am beautiful...
And I know this, generally speaking. Even at the times that I don't feel the part, God has a way of reminding me to play the part. To play MY part...and that my part doesn't include negativity and self-doubt.

I am beautiful...

Physically, my eyes are bright, my smile is wide, my thighs are curvacious and even during the winter, my skin glows *scratches back*...at the times that I don't feel "pretty" or "fly" or "fit", He sends someone along to express their admiration for my smile, eyes, my hair.

Mentally, I am stable. I am bright, charismatic, energetic, lovable, smart, funny (although cheesy at times! I love corny jokes) and always thinking... When mentally I feel a mess, and wonder, "how on EARTH am I supposed to inspire others when I can't move myself to write, workout, etc...?" God sends someone my way that is in need and allows me to give the words to encourage...

Spiritually, I am redeemed. That ALONE is enough to make me beautiful. I am in love with Christ...I am continuously gaining understanding of Christ and His life and His ministry...I have acknowledged my own calling...now to just walk in it. Obedience and wisdom.

When I feel like I belong in hell, or oh, I must already be there, God opens the door for me to tell someone about Him! ME!? Lord, You are good and Your mercy endureth forrreeeevvverrrr! Lol

I say all of this to say...I am beautiful. If I am made in the likeness of God and He is the Creator of all things, then I am a creator...I am a creator of beauty being that beauty is within me...Thank u lord.

You too, are beautiful...today and always. Try to see yourself through the eyes of God...and allow Him to use your beauty to show someone else how beautiful they are.

Loving Me & the Things I Hate About Me 2010

I hate that I'm the one to always reach out...
...that I seem to love harder than ppl seem 2 love me...
...that my heart is as big and as open as it is...and that I can't help but show it...
...that I cry over the sunrise and Kleenex commercials...
...that I am either hot or cold...
...that there is no gray area...
...that I am so expressive...
...that I oftentimes want more for others than they want for themselves...
...that I find it easier to encourage/support others more than I encourage/support myself...
...that I...
...that I still struggle with loving the things I hate about myself.

But because I realize Who created me, I am learning to love me, and all of the things I hate about me…

…because all of these things, are what make me me.

I understand that my heart is open in a world so easily closed off to the warmth of a full heart...
...that people may not know how to love…
…that maybe I can show them how…
...that God gave me arms for reaching…especially for those who pull away…

...that it's my responsibility to teach people how to love me...
...that sometimes, people want more for me than I want for myself...
...that people know they can count on me for encouragement and support...

...I am learning to love me...in spite of me. To love me just as God created me to be.

The Deception of Me 2011

I am the type to trust

Until I'm given a reason not to

Having a heart full of love for those who have

No love for me

My love is...

...pure

...honest

...consistent

I too, have been a victim of lies

I am guilty

Guilty of being loyal to those who failed to uphold me

I chose

To believe

The ones who had no more to offer than mere words

"I love…"

"You can trust…"

"I support…"

Trusting until I find myself just on the edge of bitterness

Again

Washing the taste out of my mouth with grace

A deceiver is doing what they know to do

Lies are a part of who they are

Egos the driving force in abusing others for self-gain

Convincing themselves that this is all part of the road to fame

Disillusionment is no longer an ill which ails me

Having made excuses for their victimizing

I realize that I had become a victim to the lies told by me

How I See Me 2009

Peaceful, fragrant, in love with God, knowing Him more. In a clean home that smells good…clean air, no excess of dust….one cat, maybe two…with my husband, candles burning throughout the house regularly, not cheap candles but Febreeze…Yankee even…Home Interiors…J. Crew sweaters, book tours, sharp hair…bangin' brows, healthy fit body…Ann Taylor skirts, shoes of many options. Clear skin, bright eyes, always smiling, even when I'm not…lovely voice, three children…at least…supporting my husband's business. Live shows…jazz music, traveling to see Jon in L.A., supporting Richmond Prep. Degree on wall…counseling young people…loving on them whenever they need love, which is always…long walks with my husband…closing our first home, furnishing our first home…closing our second, furnishing…warm colors in the living areas…blues and purples in the bedroom…candles…ceiling fans…book of poetry…writing daily…marathon…pain and pleasure…accomplishment…reading for enjoyment. Blue water…monthly facials…Inhale…exhale…breath deep…inhale exhale…yoga expert…Pilates warrior…I'm good…I'm toned…I'm in shape. Singing, painting…yard work…visiting girlfriends…feeding the homeless…private parties…VIP…wine connoisseur…wow, I correctly spelled connoisseur…lol laughing, loving, preaching…art on walls…fire burning…visiting family…sending them money. Giving money to strangers…taking them to eat. RL…in silver…Options…standing tall…confidence…sharing my energy…positivity. Sunday mornings…inhale exhale…fruits and veggies…healthy…bike rides in the park…FAMILY. Home in Riverside Park at home…enjoying snow in Upstate NY…healthy hands…strong hands…water fountain. Trickling water…weekends in Savannah…Charleston…NYC…Chicago…DC…LA …Some random town in the country…the will of God. Speaking at conferences…collaborating on research…in sociological journals…swimming…music makes me high…

Today 2010

Today
I'm so much better than yesterday

Dying to self daily…
Yet, living still

Only now
In God's will

Turn back?
Never will

Encouraging others
Growing still

I wasn't living before
Only existing as space to fill

Life anew
Believe He's real.

Untitled 2011

"Refocusing my heart…

…my eyes and

…my mind on God.

Realigning my vision with His will.

Repositioning myself to walk in His way.

I am being redesigned to represent the Kingdom, in a brand new way." - **2010**

Out of Blues Came the Light - 2011

"Out of the darkness that has been my night
I stand up tall, illuminated by His light.
Standing naked for all the world to see
All that God has done in me."

Queen 2011

"I am a writer who sings.

A woman who is a wife.

A sister who is a friend.

A daughter who will one day be a mother.

I am a child of God who is still growing.

I am a woman of many emotions, who chooses to love.

I am high strung and full of energy but seek peace.

I am a lover of music who also loves silence.

I love people yet appreciate solitude.

I speak often but listen closely."

Untitled 2012

Don't think I've never imagined what it's like to sleep forever

Resting peacefully in slumber until whatever is next happens

Pain has overtaken my heart in ways that are indescribable

If I could have pulled out my heart with my own hands, I would have long ago

Hatred has set a trail of fire from my soul

Burning through my eyes

At the mere sight of my own reflection

I've never hated anyone more than me

Flying without wings was impossible

Mine had been broken

Sending me falling into the deep from atop stories

This never was a good ending to mine

I've never been afraid to die but

Disappointing

Hurting

Throwing away everything You gave to me

Even when loving myself was too much to bear

My love for You has kept me alive

Miraculously washing away thoughts of suicide

By loving, You showed me how to love

Me

FOR YOU

Ginger 2011

Sister,

There's no denying that you're beautiful.

Your beauty and energy are worth more than the 6inch stilettos you wear daily to make yourself appear taller than your esteem allows you to feel

Your intelligence often overlooked

Words are ignored as your body talks through the seams of that fitted dress

Screaming to be heard

You wear stop signs as smiles

Lips painted red

Both enticing and intimidating to admirers from afar…

As a single Bumble bee

You're left feeling lonely as you buzz about

You can't sit still

In an attempt to be seen

For once

Just *be*

And be noticed

Not for the fantasy of who you are

But for the woman

You are

Maybe one day soon

You'll go beyond seeing

And notice her too

Let Them See God in You 2006

She explained to me that she truly wants to know the Lord

That she longs to be in love

With her Creator

She said, "It's hard to find Love in a world that's dominated by everything BUT God…

…or so it seems…"

But being that God IS, she has hope.

She still walks with her head held high and searches for Him wherever she goes...

She told me...

"I've *been* chasing God

I've listened to the rhythm of drums

I once thought I felt Him

As the Spirit danced along the vibrato of the voices of psalmists

I've cried, asking Him to show Himself to me

So that I can see that He is real.

Even though my mama comforted me with His Word

Enlightened me with her wisdom

And consoled me with her prayers.

I chase…

I thought I caught a glimpse of God today.
The sun was shining and even through my own clouds, I felt joy.

It had to be Him.

When it rains, I feel nurtured…

I feel tall in spite of wanting to bow down to my growing pains."

She said, "I think I saw God last night even, as artists poured out their hearts in shades of blue. I held on to every word as if God spoke them directly to me in His own thunderous voice.

She searched for Him amongst begets of Matthew, but fell asleep sometime around the begetting of David.

As I stood listening to her, I hugged her and smiled. I told her to never give up on chasing God. That He is reaching back. To keep her head held high and make sure to look others straight in the eye...

And she did. She looked me in the eye, smiled back and said, "My daddy taught me to walk with my head up, looking people directly in the eye. There you will find the
Truth."

She knows Jesus Christ the way, the truth and the life.

Can Christ be found in you?

Walk with your head held high and look others directly in the eye.

You may be the first glimpse of God that someone ever sees.

Your World Through My Eyes 2009

Some say this is the time of your life
I agree yet
Wonder if you know it
Do you know that now could make
Or break
Your life
Your will

You

I see how you yearn
You
Long for something more…
…but don't know what's missing
And search under sweaty covers
Try to cover the stench of doubt in fragrant oils
Painting over your weary smile

You rock your freak'em dress
Walking around circles
Of
Confusion
In stilettos
You try to show that you don't really care
By showing it all

You can't wash it away…trust me…
I've tried
I try...
...I can't...
I want to tell you that life

Doesn't have to be this hard
That you are what you are
Who you are
There's a voice inside
That tells you who
Who has the key to your creation
But you listen to the one that
Lies

"I know what I'm doing…"

You *are* a woman…
…You are *not* "in love" with your best sister-friend
You deserve more than what he's giving
You are more than you can imagine

Do not start this life by
loving
others
More than
You
love
yourself

How can you
Why won't you
Love yourself

And sometimes
Just listen

I have been in your world with clouded eyes
A broken heart

And a need for more

Now see your world through mine

See what can be
When I tell you that
Life doesn't have to be so hard
That
The decisions you make now…
That
I love you more than you know

I mean...
...I want you
To love you
More than you know how
And learn from the voice in your heart…
…not the one in your mind
The voices of those who
Truly
Love you

Open your eyes
As I pray for your world through mine

Aromatic Memories 2011

inhales

I inhaled long before I started breathing. Aromatic sensors taking in my surroundings

Memories of horses before I knew their names. No princess dreams of pony rides at birthday parties

We carried ice cold 45s on the ride through town on a Colt with daddy.

We never knew the danger that chased us, riding wild horses with our protector...our king.

It's ironic how the smell of liquor stores makes me smile

Bringing back happy thoughts of rides with daddy

I inhale and smile because he no longer plays Russian roulette behind wheels on Midwestern city streets.

exhales

inhales

Between sips of cola, mama took high rides...see, mommy's pony could fly.

White wings outstretched, her fantasy sprinkled with fairy dust

She lived in a world of make believe

She took great care of her white horse, lining them up with detail and devotion

Numbing her nose and the pain lingering in her heart

My inquisitiveness led by my since of smell nearly lead me to a life of addiction as I pondered what made her want to inhale…

Instead, I inhaled her…my protector, nurturer… queen

It's funny how the smell of Coca-Cola and Vanilla Musk makes me cry

Bringing back feelings of pity for the woman addicted to Coke and coke

As we rode across Midwestern highways on white horses.

I cry, because she died living a life of pain and regret…

exhales

She Loved Her So 2003

She loved her so…at the same time I cried.

Me'shell N'Degeocello was my favorite,
with her voice like mine and that smooth, Grace Jones type fade.

Yet, I cried.

Loving my boys, so boy crazy…
my leg would jump when someone grabbed at the knee,
I'd giggle as I learned that I was boy crazy…and I love men still today.

Yet…she loved her so.

They loved each other…I have my mother's smile, her cheeks but not her nose or her hai. We also share an undying love for one another…but not the same taste in men…

…for she loved her so.

When Words Mattered 2011

I remember when Words mattered

Letters used to contrive utterances were more than mere colorful rune bordering classroom blackboards and the alphabet was more than a song.

Those letters meant, opportunity was at our fingertips

Children sat bright eyed with great anticipation of learning how to build nations

Their futures were at the tips of their tongues

When words mattered

Elders taught that each generation must learn the formulas used to create the lives they never attained

The power of words were alive

As incantations spoken from the hearts like sorcerers

They spawn life and death through their words

At a time when

Coupled with a hand shake, and a look in the eye

No contracts were needed

Integrity was worth the letters it took to spell it

And the men who spoke it

Could still believe in T-R-U-S-T

A time when even the thought of someone calling my father the word used to categorize the very being that was his father was never so easily spoken from brother to brother…

From one hue to another

In the backwoods of Kentucky, they didn't call him man

"Boy" was even more a compliment compared to the word that guaranteed death was soon to follow

Not before the beatings, the tar, the feathers...the flames of hate upon the same cross that crucified our Lord.

Back when words mattered

That same hate was spelled out in the backs of our great-grands

Long before your so-called "haters" disagreed with your views

Or your actions

Or disliked your whack beats and rhymes

And said so in tweets and status updates

That word hate carried weight.

And the people who lived it, meant it, and showed that words mattered with every breath they breathed...every word spoken.

I remember thinking three words spoken in rhythm meant what they were intended to mean

"I love you" meant "I am here for you"

"I will protect you. I am all you need…"

"God is love" left no doubt in the minds of the broken hearted that true love existed

With words, the vision is made clear

The path is laid

Walk on the words spoken

Creating the world only yet seen in the imagination

Words

Matter

New Strange Fruit 2009

Today there is a new strange fruit

Mothers and grandmothers still send their sons and daughters out into the world

Leaving themselves alone to their worry

"Will my son be okay?"

"Will my baby girl make it home to me today?

But see, strange fruit no longer hangs from trees

If falls from branches

Broken and weakened by generations of family roots

Planted in bad soil

The next generation growing up from beneath the same tree like weeds

Fighting and pressing their way through cracks in concrete in city streets

We are a new strange fruit

But instead of descendents of Robert E. Lee

Our fruit is being plucked by hands topped with chocolate like me

We are a new strange fruit

A Small Poem for Black Men 2008

I loved you before Obama
before Jordan and Miles
Even after white boys tried to bite your style
I loved you before my father gave up his Colt
Even in him, I saw so much hope
I love my Black man
Your power divine
And I thank you for loving me
It's our time to shine!

Sisters.

Let today be a day that no matter what you're wearing

What your hair may look like or

What size you may be

YOU *FEEL* BEAUTIFUL!

Beauty begins where everything else begins...IN THE MIND!

Look at all the beauty around you in the world & let it BECOME you! Take it all!

Brothers.

Do the same!

Let the power of the wind, sun and rain IGNITE a new fire of strength within you!

Look all around. Nature emulates your strength.

God created you to take dominion over the earth. Let today be the day that you tap into the power that you have within!"

– June, 2010

Essays

How I Got Over Him 2005

This is an old blog but very timely in today's discussion regarding love and grace. A young sister came to me today asking about a two year committed relationship recently ended, what seemed to her to be, abruptly.

This lesson doesn't just pertain to former romantic relationships but relationships in general.
It is always my prayer that my experiences and lessons learned bless the lives of someone else.

Wednesday, September 28, 2005
I have a sister who asked me to pray for her that she would get her mind off of "him". She said she's prayed and prayed about it herself and I realized that I had went through the same thing with my own "him" a few years back and as I was speaking this to her, it ministered to me as well:

If you're gonna pray for the Lord to take your mind off of a person or thing, pray it once, call it done and move it forward. It didn't make sense for me to keep going to God sayin, "oh Lord...blah, blah, blah, take my mind off him." By continuously doing that, my mind was still on HIM!? (the very person I was "praying" I'd get over...)

Instead...to truly find peace, take more time to worship God. Tell God how amazing He is, how wonderful, how merciful. Thank Him for the good times and the lessons learned.

When we get involved in relationships, we tend to give ALL of our energy, time and emotions to that individual and to making it WORK with that individual. If God were truly our priority, we would take the time to worship and praise God, that way we won't even be thinking about worshipping and praising him/her.

Nothing and no one deserves all of my energy/emotions BUT God!

My favorite Scripture in life right now...Matt 6:33: "Seek ye first the Kingdom of God and His righteousness and all things will be added unto you."

Pruning and Purging 2010

To all of you dealing w/the purging of "friends" in your life, again I remind you that you are not alone in this purging season. A plentiful harvest cannot come forth without properly purging. The harvest you've been expecting from your sowing is coming forth. Be prepared to receive it! If you hold on to what God is trying to remove, you won't have room to receive what He has for you! MAKE ROOM in your life for the promises of God to come to fruition!

Be mindful, when you are purging to not be too rough on the pieces you're removing! Those pieces may not be dead totally and can be revived later with time and proper care. Just like with pruning a plant...there may be a piece that was too weak to help the whole plant grow, but on its own, it can flourish, becoming a whole new plant later in life. Relationships are the same way. Some may not be healthy for your growth NOW, but in the future, they may be a vital part of your life.

So, as you prune and purge, do not do so with a spiteful heart. Always walk in love and grace. I am glad to say that I am still friends with many who, at one point, were removed from my life! No distaste or bitterness involved!

I give thanks to God for allowing my life and my experiences to help you overcome! He is so good!

The Habit of Disappointment 2010

I woke up feeling quite disappointed in myself. From my excessive use of blue cheese dressing to my failure to write consistently, I've been slippin'...

Layered in between the blue cheese and my loss of significant use of words you can find too much sleep and not enough prayer. Over-eating and lack of cardio...

It is believed that it takes 21 days to form a new habit - whether that habit be good or bad. I have found this to be true, which is why it is detrimental to our continued growth that we not "wait til Monday" to go back to the gym or the beginning of the month to start eating right.

If it takes 21 days for a new habit to be formed, NOW is as crucial as ever. Although I woke up disappointed for various reason, I can't allow myself to remain disappointed for too long. NOW, not tomorrow, not next week, NOW is the time to take an honest assessment, shake off the disappointment and keep it moving.

"There is therefore now no condemnation to those who are in Christ Jesus, who do not walk according to the flesh, but according to the Spirit."

Romans 8:1 shares a great promise to those who are in Christ. Now to just STOP walking according to my flesh...self-control in every area...

Every day that we wallow in what we didn't do yesterday is throwing God's gift of today back in His face!

TODAY is what we have. Shake of the habits that keep you bound in disappointment and GO FORTH in the gifts of grace and mercy that we receive with each new day!

The Monster Within 2010

Do you recall your first brush with fear? Was it a nightmare interrupting your slumber, awaking you to the possibilities of monsters under the bed? Or the loud crack of thunder accompanied by a bright, shining sword extending its' blade through the sky? Whatever it was, in our youth, the idea of the unknown sent many of us into a frenzy either frozen under the covers with our eyes tightly shut or down the hall seeking sanctuary in the room of an older sibling or our parents. Even in the presence of someone bigger and stronger than us, the eyes that peered through the darkness from the confines of the closet were brighter than our own eyes in the sunshine and at this point in our lives, fear of all things unfamiliar begins to tighten its' grip on our imagination.

On the other hand, the innocence of a child is also laced with wisdom. As children we have confidence in our abilities in the light and many children are fearless and willing to take on whatever the day brings be it an 8 ft tree to climb, a wide creek to jump or a small clan of bullies to stand up to on the playground, their strength and courage is magnified in the presence of light.

If children can display unmatched bravery in the face of adversity, how much harder should it be for us as adults to get over the fears that ridicule us day in and day out? It is quite natural to fear the unknown but if we are children of God, having received He who is Love and have the Spirit within us through the life of Christ, there is no reason to live according to the uncertainty of darkness.

Chapter Four of First John helps us to see the confidence that we have in the Light…in Love…in God. Verse 13 "We know that we live in Him and He in us, because He has given us of His Spirit…16 And so we know and rely on the love God has for us. God is love. Whoever lives in love lives in God, and God in him…18 There is no fear in love. But perfect love drives out fear…"

The world has no need of seeking to conquer us with fear when our own imaginations leave us entrapped in a nightmare as life becomes the monsters in our closets. With the love of God, who is love, all things are possible. His perfect love drives out fear.

"…I need your help, save me from myself; I've been running from me all along. I don't know what I will make of my life, if you don't right all my wrongs…I've been running for so long yet I'm not getting anywhere…can you please come rescue me from this nightmare…I feel like I'm running…I'm so tired of running…" – ***Leah Smith, Monsters from Beautifully Made, 2009***

Ignoring is Ignorance 2011

Acknowledging issues is the first step to overcoming them. Contrary to popular belief, ignoring things/people does NOT make them go away. Unopened mail, ignored phone calls and necessary conversations just prolongs the process to recovery and liberation.

When u think about it, ignoring unresolved issues is a form of cowardice and shows a lack of maturity and for the "Believer", allowing issues to go unresolved shows a lack of faith that all things do indeed "work together for the good..."

Do not be fooled. Handle your business and get on with business.

Speaking of Haters…STOP Speaking of Haters 2011

Many don't have "enemies" or haters as we suspect. There may be people who disagree with or don't choose to support you for whatever reason.

In all actuality, there's but one enemy and although he may use people to distract/discourage/discredit you, HE'S the enemy, not his pawns. The good thing about THAT enemy is that, he's already been DEFEATED!

…the bad thing is, because our enemy HAS been defeated, you can no longer use him or his pawns as an excuse for not succeeding or making progress as it relates to your dreams and/or God given vision.

I recently saw someone on Twitter say that they use haters as their motivation. I, personally, wouldn't use "haters" as my motivation. Pleasing & glorifying God is my motivation, inspiring others is my motivation…

Stop giving the enemy and his pawns so much power by constantly speaking of them…especially if said haters don't *really* exist…

If people don't support/believe in u, it's okay. That doesn't mean they're hating on you…There's an "audience" for everyone and plenty of support to go around.

Wait and prepare for God given, divine connections! If we truly spend our time seeking "...first the Kingdom of God..." our sights/minds won't have time to be on all the potential distractions.

Our dreams have not been deferred; our vision has just been blurred.

Lord, bring focus to the lives of all who read this (and those who don't...). I pray that we keep our hearts and minds focused on You and all You've called us to do! AMEN!

Quiet My Clamorous Mind 2012

This morning I was reminded of why it is important to pray before turning to sleep for the night. As long as we're alive, our mind is constantly working. Doubt, fear and disbelief hit me hard while I sleep. These things creep in when I'm not consciously able to confront them with the Word or awake to declare the promises of God.

Too many times I've awaken out of my slumber to find myself overwhelmed with worry. This is why the Word MUST BE IN US and we must seek to dwell on it day and night.

We must meditate on His Word and the promises within so that even in our sleep, we worship and God can/will be magnified in our hearts and minds.

"Praying without ceasing" is real and *necessary* in the life of the believer! Align your spirit with that of God and peace will sustain you, even while you sleep.

Spirit vs. Stars
What Rules You? 2012

Hi...my name is Nina, and I'm a Cancer. In this truth, I recognize that I am an emotional, sensitive, energetic, loving, nurturing being who has been known to hide in a hard shell (in my case, a shell of sarcasm) when trouble arises instead of dealing with my emotions. I'm that sister who seems to have it together and be strong when really, I'm the type to cry over anything and my feelings get hurt, easily.

"Cancer motto could be, "A good defense is the best offense." Like a Crab in its cave, your attack can consist of baiting your opponent into your territory. What appears to be a retreat to others can be your best aggressive tactic. As you feel your way through life, building your security by developing your home and family relationships, remember that unexpressed anger can turn into resentment and depression, so find someone you can trust and share your feelings."

"Cancer - Your Biggest Strength: Your ability to nurture others
Your Potential Weakness: Fear of the past repeating in the future"

Hi...my name is Nina and I'm a follower of Christ and am filled with His Spirit. Because of **THIS** truth, I am learning that I must make a CONSCIOUS effort to walk according to the Spirit, NOT the stars.

Even when dealing with the most painful feelings, I am learning to walk in love, patience, kindness...to suffer long...to practice self-control (to include emotional responsibility). This is not always easy considering I've always been encouraged to express myself. In my adult life, I still find myself seeking a balance between the best and the worst parts of me. This is when walking according to the Spirit is ever more important.

[22] But the fruit of the Spirit is love, joy, peace, longsuffering, kindness, goodness, faithfulness, [23] gentleness, self-control. Against such there is no law. [24] And those who are Christ's have crucified the flesh with its passions and desires. [25] If we live in the Spirit, let us also walk in the Spirit. [26] Let us not become conceited, provoking one another, envying one another.

Math bears truth - Two plus two does indeed equal four.

Science bears truth - Gravity is REAL.

The moon circles the earth. Its pull raises the tide. Its cycle works within women of a certain age.

This is *truth*.

Astrology bears truth. The stars continuously align while time as we know it continues on and with those alignments, energies from outside of us play a part in being who God created us to be.

The difference between Nina who is a Cancer and Nina who is a child of God is the Truth that I CHOOSE to *live* according to. No horoscope is going to tell me how my day is going to go when I live according to plan greater than what our natural mind can comprehend.

Just because my mind doesn't fully understand the equations that make up mathematics, doesn't make their outcome any less TRUE.

Knowing that my life does indeed align with the stars within Cancer, I also know that my emotions cycle with the moon and that they ebb and flow as the water. In knowing *this* truth I also know that I must make a concerted effort to not allow the stars to rule me but to always be ruled by the Spirit.

Let us not make excuses for our emotional irresponsibility. Just as people use the Word to justify their behaviors and ideals, women have been known to use PMS to act like the devil once a month and people use the zodiac to their advantage…or the disadvantage of others.

puts on churchy voice Choose ye this day...what will you allow to rule you?
http://www.huffingtonpost.com/horoscopes/astrology/cancer/about/

...Much is Given 2013

Although gaining financial wealth has always been a driving force in prosperity, I have personally seen a recent rise in the number of people who seem to be pushing towards making a dream come true for the sake of fortune and fame.

I have found myself growing weary of supporting people I see hustling their talents for money. Even as indie artists, it's possible to pimp oneself just as much as industry execs. Many who have been driven by the need to make money off of their vision without understanding the greater purpose in creating have found that their hasty efforts were in vain often rushing projects to get them in the hands of whomever they think will be interested and in turn, putting out mediocre work!

Putting out a product, be it a CD, book, a piece of fine art or even a service without ensuring it's your best work is not only a waste money, time and energy but can also potentially tarnish the name/brand that you worked "so hard" at establishing. Then when the product doesn't gain popularity as hoped, people will scream that "people don't support their own!" Well, who do YOU know wants to endorse mess!?

I am learning that there will always be people who are willing to support your vision. The key is

> **actually having a vision and not just an idea! Many don't know the difference between the two!!!**

This behavior is especially troubling when I see it displayed by those who consider themselves to be believers of Christ. Lord knows that the current condition of the economy has people seeking to create multiple streams of income to support themselves and their families but our inability to focus on the will of God for our gifts/talents/ministry is merely tossing our seeds about which never generates a fruitful harvest.

> **"A farmer went out to sow his seed. ⁴ As he was scattering the seed, some fell along the path, and the birds came and ate it up. ⁵ Some fell on rocky places, where it did not have much soil. It sprang up quickly, because the soil was shallow. ⁶ But when the sun came up, the plants were scorched, and they withered because they had no root. ⁷ Other seed fell among thorns, which grew up and choked the plants. ⁸ Still other seed fell on good soil, where it produced a crop..." Matthew 13:4-8**

I have been asked me why I do so many speaking engagements/gigs for free. The answer is simple: **I give much because much as been given TO me**. My talents, time and energy all serve a purpose greater than me. I dare not do what I do with the mere goal of making money. I seek to fulfill my God given purpose and in doing so, KNOW and EXPECT that prosperity WELL BEYOND MONEY will come to me and my family.

If your "grind" has you focused on "making it" or "making money", you need to readjust your focus on PURPOSE. Your gift will truly make room for you but we must **"...seek ye first the Kingdom of God..."** Y'all know how it goes!

One day (soon possibly), I'll get paid for all that I do but for now, the bank of my heart is filled with gratitude that God sees fit to use ME at all! The payoff I receive from knowing that people are blessed by my words and even my presence is greater than the checks that will come!

**"For everyone to whom much is given, from him much will be required;
and to whom much has been committed, of him they will ask the more." Luke 12:48**

Quotes and Thoughts

Love Walk

"Why shouldn't I lose sleep to begin walking IN my dreams...? I never remember the dreams that I have when I sleep anyway...Now begins the time to stay awake in order to make my dreams become reality."

"It's not you, it's me." As much as people dislike hearing this when it comes to the shifting or even the demise of relationships, I've often found it to be true. It's not you, it's me. It's me trying to move forward...it's me growing. It's me getting over my insecurities. It's me learning to love me. "No really...It's not you, it's me."

"It's not enough to say we believe in something if we don't choose to act on it..."

"Instead of crying every time your feelings get hurt even a little bit, apply a little grace and keep it moving. Unless someone is truly tearing you down and blatantly being malicious, don't allow the lack of phone calls/texts/visits determine whether YOU are a good friend to someone or whether they are a true friend to you."

"If you're ever embarrassed by or disappointed in your actions or behavior, *change* your actions/behavior. Avoiding damage is easier than damage control. I learned that lesson the hard way while I've found myself apologizing for my actions more than any one person should.

"There will be drama today...conflicting forces are all around us! Focus your heart, attention and *intentions* on the correct force!"

"I am excited for tomorrow when I will be better than I am today! In the meanwhile, I'm SO glad for today, now that I'm better than I was yesterday!"

"Be mindful of the memories you make. One day, you may wish you could forget them."

"Everyone has the power to influence. The question is what are you doing with your influence?"

I choose wisely, to release those who do not know how or refuse to do so, from the obligation of loving me...yet, I love freely.

No matter what happens today, walk in love! Do not go looking for disappointment, particularly in people...expect LOVE and receive LOVE! Expect the best out of people & if for some reason they fail to meet your expectations, *that* is the best opportunity to display the love you say you have!

**"I was raised in unconventional homes yet imbued in unconditional love.
Because of this, I find myself loving unconventionally, pouring out love unconditionally."**

Remember, just because some*one* doesn't think you're important/special {enough} doesn't make you any less important/special. Know your self-worth.

Love for a person is like water to a plant...love me as I am and watch me grow...If you don't like something about someone...love them anyway. Your love inspires them to continue growing...

Balance in life: Don't get caught up in giving all the love and taking how others treat you if it's less than what you need. That's not healthy in *any* relationship. That's not to say you should go crying over everything but at some point, people need to know the how we feel. People will only treat us the way we *let* them treat us.

Never regret the seeds you've sown, regardless of your current relationship with the PEOPLE you've sown into. People change, the principles of God do not. Sowing = Reaping...ALWAYS. This is why discernment is important in every area of our lives, particularly where we sow our seeds.

In the past, I've failed to use discernment, finding myself supporting people who only kept me around for free "labor"/promotion & their ego's sake. It's a terrible shame because we WANT to build solid relationships, especially w/those who SEEM to be about Kingdom building.

Looking back, sometimes, our desire to be "needed" is an ego trip of our own. This keeps a lot of people in both professional and personal relationships that they have no business being in!

repeats Mind over matter. I have the mind of Christ over the matters of this world.

"I have stood tall in the presence of God and bowed in worship at His feet...NO MAN or WOMAN on this entire Earth is so great that I cannot be in their presence. GOD goes before me wherever He leads. Walk in confidence onto the path that God has prepared for you! Fear NO MAN..."

He said: "[a good woman] recognizes that her love has great value and must be reciprocated. If her love is taken for granted, it soon disappears."

To which I replied:
"Even when others don't value my love and give it in return, my love is not mine to keep. I will always give it freely."

Never withhold your love but find a place for those who fail to love you as you need to be loved.

It's "funny" the way God prepares us for what He's called us to...sometimes, it *hurts* and many times, frightening. The pain and uncertainty of this walk is why it is *imperative* that we keep our sight and hearts on God FIRST...ALWAYS. Our inability to do so can RUIN our walk/ministry and everyone connected to it.

About the Author

Nina C. Brewton is a mentor, speaker and vocalist who seeks to inspire others in all she does. The native of Wichita, Kansas is a veteran of the United States Air Force and currently lives in Hampton, Virginia with her husband Raphael.

From large assemblies to intimate classroom settings, Mrs. Brewton is available to speak at your school, church, conference or private function.

She is the author of a memoir, *Dramas of a Bald Head Queen* and is working on a tribute to sisterhood, *Sangin' Like Shug Avery*.

For more info or booking, visit www.baldheadqueen.com

www.ingramcontent.com/pod-product-compliance
Lightning Source LLC
Chambersburg PA
CBHW071306040426
42444CB00009B/1887